W9-BBZ-441

Snap books® Girl Talk

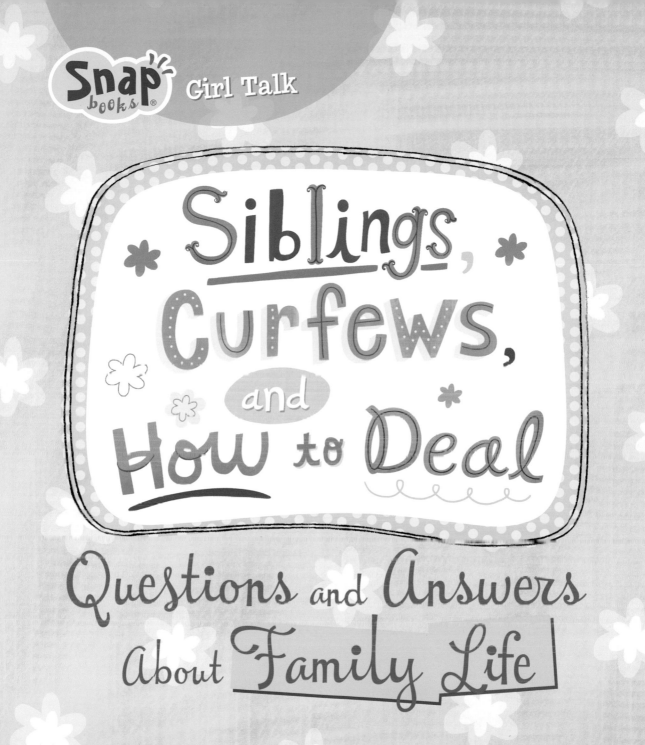

Siblings, Curfews, and How to Deal

Questions and Answers About Family Life

by Nancy Loewen and Paula Skelley
illustrated by Julissa Mora

CAPSTONE PRESS
a capstone imprint

Content adviser:
John E. Desrochers, PhD

Table of Contents

Isabella   Lan   Claudia   Sagal

What do you think of when you hear the word

"family"?

Do you think of brothers or sisters? One parent or two? How about grandparents, aunts, uncles, and cousins? Maybe you think of your dog or hamster as part of the family. Families come in all shapes and sizes. No two are exactly alike. But the one thing they all have is love.

Families aren't always easy.

Just when you think you've got things figured out, something changes. Brothers and sisters get on your nerves. Parents divorce or remarry or have more kids. Grandparents get sick or move away.

SOMETIMES YOU DON'T WANT ANYTHING TO DO WITH YOUR FAMILY.

 At other times you can't wait to tell them about your day.

If you have questions about family life,

you've come to the right place!

We know what you're going through. Share your concerns, and we'll share our best advice. And if you still can't figure it out, be sure to talk to a trusted adult.

Q Lately I'd rather talk to my mom than my dad. Is that OK?

A Sure! Just because you have more to say to your mom right now doesn't mean you love your dad any less. It might be easier to talk about things like clothes or body changes or girlfriend troubles with your mom. She's been through it. But you should still find ways to connect with your dad. Work on a project together. Or have a dad-and-daughter date at a special restaurant. Maybe one day it'll be easier to talk to your dad about some things than your mom. That's OK too. People grow and change and so do their relationships.

Q What should I do when my dad tells me to do one thing and my mom tells me to do something else?

A It's confusing when parents aren't on the same page. But it happens in every family at one time or another. Let your parents know they told you different things. Then give them a chance to work it out. Don't just follow whichever instructions you like better.

If your parents aren't around to set things straight, you'll have to decide for yourself. Trust your instincts and make the best decision you can, but talk to your parents as soon as possible.

Do these mix-ups happen a lot? Do your mom and dad always argue about parenting stuff? Ask them to write down their rules or find a better way to let you know what's going on.

Q If my parents aren't home, I can't have friends over. Not even my next-door neighbor! How can I convince my parents that the house won't fall down just because they aren't there?

A Ask your parents to make a list of the things you need to do in order to have a friend over while they are out. Prove to them that you are responsible by following the family rules. Do you clean up after yourself? Do you let the dog out? Do you turn off lights and close windows and put food away and all that? Do you know who to call if something goes wrong?

See if your parents will say yes to a few "practice runs." Let them decide how long you and your friend can be alone. If everything goes OK, they may change their rules.

Tip Clip

When your parents tell you no, don't sulk or complain. If you stay calm and cool, you'll show them that you're growing up.

A Your dad wants you to be the best you can be. He probably doesn't realize that his comments aren't helping you do better—they're discouraging you from trying. Be honest and calmly tell him how you feel. Be honest with yourself too. If you aren't putting in a good effort, admit it.

Maybe your dad will get it. Maybe he won't. But if you know that you did your best, you can be proud of yourself no matter what.

Q My mom went back to work, and now everything is different. I have a lot more chores, and I can't do as many activities because she can't pick me up. Why can't she be just a mom again?

A Because she's not JUST a mom. She's a person too!

Is she working because your family needs the money? Is she working because she loves what she does? Either way, she's doing what she needs to do. Sure, change is tough, but you'll get used to it in time.

If there's a certain activity you really want to keep doing, see if your dad or an aunt or uncle can drive you. Or ask your parents to look into carpooling.

Q My dad is awesome, but I'm embarrassed to bring my friends home because he doesn't speak English. What should I do?

A You already said your dad's awesome, so really, what's there to be embarrassed about? Bridge the gap between your dad and your friends. Teach him some basic words to say to your friends. Ask him to teach you and your friends some things to say in his language. Just seeing you and your dad together will help your friends see how great he is—even if they don't speak the same language.

7

Making Time

 My parents are super-busy. It's like they never have time to do anything fun as a family. Any suggestions?

Tell your parents you want more family time. Once they know how important it is to you, maybe they'll cut back on some of their other activities.

Keep a list of fun things you can do together that don't take a lot of time. How about a quick game of cards, a bike ride, or a picnic supper in the park? How about watching funny YouTube videos? Or pick some "family only" days every month—everyone agrees not to make other plans on those days.

Even ordinary tasks can be fun if everyone's got the right attitude. Go grocery shopping together. Wash the car. Paint the living room! It's about spending time together, not what you do.

I wish I could spend more time with my mom, without my little brother tagging along. Is there anything I can do about it?

Little brothers and sisters are great, but so is time alone with your mom. It might take some planning though. Talk to your mom about ways to find more "girl time" together. Plan an at-home mani-pedi during one of his naps. Invite your mom to watch a movie with you after your little brother goes to bed for the night. Maybe your brother could have some special time with another family member while you have time with your mom.

How do I tell my parents they've scheduled me for too many activities?

Decide which activities are the most important to you. What do you enjoy most? Make a list of the reasons you chose them. If you think it through, your parents will know you are serious and not just having a bad week. Pick a time when you can talk without being interrupted. Explain that you're feeling stressed out and need to cut back on your activities. Who knows, they might like having more time at home too.

Q My sister has ADHD and never gets around to doing things she's supposed to do. Why do I have to be responsible when she doesn't have to be?

A Having ADHD means that her brain works differently than yours does. It's a big challenge to make herself do things she's not interested in (like helping around the house). Your sister probably wishes she were more like you. Be proud of how responsible you are. Don't worry about what she's doing or not doing—that's between your sister and your parents. One thing you CAN do is encourage her. Tell her she did a great job cleaning her room. Ask if she will help you do the dishes. Doing chores together might help her stay focused on what needs to be done. She'll try harder if she feels her family is on her side.

Q My younger brother drives me crazy, following and copying me. I need breathing space! What can I do?

A That doesn't sound like much fun for either of you! Instead of always trying to get away from your brother, give him some of your time. Tell him you'll play a game with him, but when you're done playing, you'll get to do your own thing. Or set up a "play date," just like you would if he were a friend and not your little brother. When the play date is over, you get time to yourself. Try to stick to a routine, so he'll know what to expect. And if your brother still gets in your way too much, ask your parents for help.

Q: How can I stop fighting with my brother and sister?

A: Arguing can become a habit. A bad habit! To break it, pay attention to your thoughts and feelings. Are you mad at your sister or are you in a bad mood about something else? Does it really matter if your brother gets to use the computer before you do?

If you fight about the same things all the time, talk about it when you are getting along. See if there's a fair way to handle your problems. If you fight about where to sit in the car, take turns

If you ever get really mad—so mad that you feel like hitting—go to another room. Calm yourself down by taking some deep breaths. Listen to some music. Watch something funny on TV or online.

Brothers and sisters argue. They just do. But if arguing turns into physical fighting, that's not cool. Neither is name-calling or saying mean things to hurt someone's feelings. Ask your parents for help before things get out of hand.

Q: I heard my parents talking about my older sister's curfew last night. What's a curfew? Should I have one too?

A: A curfew is a kind of house rule. It's a specific time that someone has to be back home. Parents use curfews to help keep track of when kids will be home—and to keep them safe. If you break a curfew, you might be grounded or lose certain privileges. Chances are, if your sister has a curfew, one day you will too.

Honesty and Trust

Q I saw my sister steal money from my mom's purse. Should I tell?

A Talk to your sister first. Are you sure she STOLE the money? Maybe your mom gave her permission to take it. If your sister did steal the money, give her a chance to tell your mom what she did. If your sister won't admit it, though, you should definitely tell your mom. Then let her handle the situation. You did the right thing, and now it's between the two of them.

Q I lied to my dad, and now he doesn't trust me. How do I win back his trust?

A By being honest, all the time. No matter what. Even when it's hard, tell your dad the truth. No little white lies either! Don't tell him you ate your broccoli if you put it down the garbage disposal. It will take some time to win back his trust. There aren't any shortcuts.

Q I accidentally broke Mom's special vase from her grandmother, and then I hid it. How can I tell her? I'm scared!

A It will be hard, but tell your mom before she finds out. Explain what happened and apologize. Write a note if you feel more comfortable doing that. Accidents happen, but hiding the vase was wrong. Your mom might get mad. And she might punish you. But she'll get over it, and so will you. Offer to pay for the vase with your own money. If it can't be replaced, you could make your mom something special that reminds her of her grandmother. If an accident like this happens again, be honest about it right away.

Tip Clip

Trust is super-important for good relationships. Being trustworthy is hard work sometimes, but it's worth it!

House Rules

Q Some kids in my class watch movies that are PG-13, but my mom says I have to be 13 before I can watch them. I'm 9 and think I am old enough. What do you think?

A Movies are rated PG-13 for a reason. Some stuff in those movies isn't meant for kids. Some kids might act cool because they saw a certain movie. But maybe they were more scared than they let on. Your mom is following the rules. She also knows you and what you're ready for. So wait until you're 13. There are plenty of good movies to see that are meant just for you.

Q Why won't my parents let me have a TV or computer in my room? Everyone else has one!

A It might SEEM like all the other kids have TVs or computers in their rooms, but a lot of kids don't. You're not the only one.

Ask your parents to explain the reasons behind their rule. Maybe they're worried you'll stay up too late or watch things you're not ready for. Maybe they want you to read more or spend time on more creative things, like drawing or writing. Maybe they can't afford it. Keep in mind they just want to do what's best for you.

Q My older sister has a cell phone. I want one too, but my parents say I'm too young. How can I convince them to give me one?

A Show your parents how responsible you can be. If you lose things or drop stuff a lot, maybe a cell phone isn't such a good idea. Are you helping out at home? Getting your homework done? Keeping your room clean? If you do a good job with those things, you'll have a better shot at getting a cell phone.

Even if you do everything right, your parents still might say no. Cell phones can be expensive. Your parents may need to know you're totally ready for one before spending the money. Hang in there.

Q My dads always complain that I spend too much time watching TV or playing computer games. But all my friends spend just as much time on the computer as I do! How much screen time is too much?

A That depends. TV and computer games are fun, but they make time disappear. You need to do other activities too. Do you spend time outside? Read books and get your homework done? Do you hang out with your friends in person? Are you getting enough sleep? Your dads might be worried that you don't spend enough time doing these kinds of things.

Talk to your dads and come up with a schedule for your screen time. Then stick to it! If they see that you're able to stick to the schedule, they'll feel better. And so will you.

 *Tip Clip*

Write down your family's rules, and keep them where family members can see them. Review them once in a while so you don't forget.

Q My mom and dad are getting a divorce. I'm so mad at both of them. How can they do this to me?

A It's totally normal to feel angry when your parents divorce. It's a huge change in your life, and you can't do anything about it. But remember that your parents don't want to hurt you. This is a decision between them. And it wasn't an easy one.

Sometimes life is hard. That's just the way it is. If time goes by and you still have a rough time dealing with the divorce, tell your parents. Try to be specific about what makes you angry and sad. Maybe it's that you have to live in two places now or that you miss Sunday morning pancakes. If you need more help, see if your parents can find a support group that's just for kids. Talking to a counselor or other kids going through the same thing can help you feel better.

Q My dad moved out, and I only get to see him every other weekend. What if he forgets about me?

A You're his daughter, and there's no way he could ever forget about you. You won't forget about him, will you?

Things will change, but you can stay connected if you try. Talk to your dad and figure out ways to stay in touch during the times you're apart. Have phone calls or video chats together. Write letters, e-mails, or texts. You can even play games together online. Save your school papers and go through them with your dad when you visit him. You won't see your dad at home every day anymore, but you can still be close.

Q How do I tell my friends that my parents are getting a divorce? It's embarrassing.

A Lots of families go through a divorce. There's no reason to be embarrassed. You didn't do anything wrong.

Confide in one or two close friends. Get used to the idea of having others know. When you're ready to tell your other friends and classmates, it's OK to keep it short and simple. If kids ask you questions you don't want to answer, explain that you'd rather not talk about it.

Tip Clip

Give yourself time to adjust to the "new normal" after your parents' divorce. It's a big change, but eventually you will get used to it.

My parents are splitting up, and my brothers and I feel like it's our fault somehow. How can we get them back together?

When parents split up or get a divorce, it's because they had problems. It's about them, not you or anything you did or didn't do. And no matter how much you might want to get them back together, it's not a good idea. That stuff is just between your parents. The best thing you can do is respect your parents' decisions and let them know how much you love them.

Part of the week I live with my dad, and part of the week I live with my mom. How am I supposed to keep track of all my stuff?

Lists can be a big help. Work with your parents to make a list of the things you will need to take with you every time. Make another list that's just for the current visit—things like library books, a sports uniform, or supplies for a school project. Before you leave one house, go through both lists to make sure you have everything. Keep your things together, so it will be easier to find them when it's time to go. If your parents are willing, you could get two sets of the items you need all the time, like toothbrushes or pajamas. That way you won't have to take them back and forth every time.

Q My dad remarried, and now I have an instant stepbrother. How am I supposed to treat a stranger like a brother?

A

Instant families aren't easy. Your new stepbrother may feel the same way. Treat him as you would a new friend. Play games together to break the ice. Find out what you both like to do. Pretty soon you'll get used to each other, and things won't feel so strange. Someday you might even become close enough to feel like brother and sister. If not, that's OK. You still gained a friend.

Q My mom has a new husband and a new kid too. What if she likes her new stepdaughter more than she likes me?

A You're still your mom's daughter, right? She still loves you. That didn't change. Tell yourself that you don't need to compete with your stepsister. Repeat when necessary! Try to get to know your stepsister. You are family now too.

When you and your mom are alone, it's OK to share your worries and fears. If you're too shy to come out and say it, write her a note. Make plans to keep spending one-on-one time with your mom, doing the things you like to do together. Be confident in your mom's love—and in yourself.

Q My dad is expecting a baby with his new wife. I'm excited but worried too. What if the new baby takes him away from me?

A Babies are a lot of work. Your dad will be busy and tired, and he might not have a lot of time for you at first. That doesn't mean he loves you less. As the baby gets older, things will get easier. Later on, if you need to spend more time with your dad, tell him. And when you see your dad having fun with the new baby, remember that he once did those things with you. Enjoy your new stepsister or stepbrother, and know that no one can ever take your place in your dad's life.

Q Since the divorce, Mom and Dad always fight when they pick up and drop off my sister and me. We don't like it. What can we do?

A It's hard to be caught in the middle. But your words may help. Tell your parents that their fighting bothers you. Ask them to stop.

Are the drop-offs and pick-ups happening at home? If so, could you meet in a public place next time, like at a restaurant or mall? If there are a lot of people around, your parents probably won't fight so much.

If things get really bad, talk to other family members or another adult you trust. You shouldn't have to deal with your parents fighting.

Q I really like my new stepdad, but I'm worried about hurting my dad's feelings. What should I do?

A When you're with your dad, don't talk a lot about your stepdad. You don't need to hide anything, but just enjoy the time with your dad. Your dad might feel left out sometimes, but you can't change that. Liking your stepdad is not being disloyal to your dad. The main thing is, your dad wants you to be happy. He knows that getting along with your stepdad is good for you and your whole family.

Q I don't agree with any of my new stepmother's rules. Dad says I have to follow them anyway. Do I really have to?

A Yes, you do have to follow your stepmother's rules. But think through why you don't agree with them. Is it really about the rules or is it more about your stepmother? Have an honest talk with your dad. See if you can come up with a plan you can all live with.

It can be hard to accept someone new in your dad's life. But there must be something good about your stepmother—your dad married her, after all. Give her a chance, and try to open up around her.

Ask questions about her favorite movies, TV shows, or sports teams. Share your favorite music or foods. Tell her something funny that one of your friends did. Things should get easier when you and your stepmother know each other better.

My grandma is very sick. She might die soon. How should I act around her?

Let your grandma be your guide. If she wants to rest, sit with her and hold her hand. If she feels like company, you can talk, sing, or even read to her. She will enjoy hearing all about your life—your art project at school, the book you just finished reading, a party you're going to, and things like that. If she's well enough, make a memory book together.

Your grandma might look different than she used to, and that can be kind of scary. Be brave. She is still the same person inside—someone who is important to you and cares about you a lot.

If your grandma does pass away, it will be hard. But remembering all the good times you had together will help you feel better.

We moved because my mom got a new job. My old house was just down the street from my grandparents. My new house is three states away! How can I stay close to my grandparents now that we're so far apart?

 Just because you live far away doesn't mean you and your grandparents have to grow apart. There are lots of ways to stay in touch. Do your grandparents have a computer or tablet? You could video chat with them. That way you could show them your new puppy, play piano for them, or share your latest spelling test. If your grandparents aren't into technology, you can always talk to them on the phone. Writing letters can be fun too. Ask if you can visit them when you're on a school break.

Tip Clip

Don't take your loved ones for granted. Make the most of the time you spend with each other. The good memories you create will be with you the rest of your life.

I see my grandparents only once or twice a year. They don't have much to say to me. What can we talk about?

 It sounds like you need to get to know each other better. Sometimes it's easier to talk to people when you're doing other things. Play board games, bake cookies, or make an art project with your grandparents. Go to a library or museum together.

If it's hard to get your grandparents to open up, try asking them questions about their lives. Pretend you're writing an article about them for the school paper or a class assignment. Ask to see old photos. If you're still having trouble, ask your parents for ideas to help you and your grandparents connect.

Q I really like hanging out with my aunt. She's super-fun, and we do things that my mom and I never do together. Why can't my mom be fun like her sister?

A It's cool that you get along so well with your aunt. But everybody's different. Think about you and your friends. Do you all like exactly the same things? Do you have exactly the same abilities? Maybe your aunt just has a more outgoing personality. Maybe she doesn't have as many responsibilities as your mom does. Maybe she has more money to do things. Plus, she's your aunt, not your mom. She doesn't have to do all the everyday things your mom does for you.

It's great your mom lets you spend time with your aunt. Next time invite your mom to come along. You might see a different side of her when she's with her sister.

Tip Clip

Gifts from the heart are awesome. Your parents, grandparents, aunts, and uncles will love getting anything from you, like letters, pictures, crafts, and baked goods. You don't need a special occasion.

Money

Q My parents give me an allowance, but sometimes I don't have any money left at the end of the week. Shouldn't my parents just give me money when I need it? My friends' parents do.

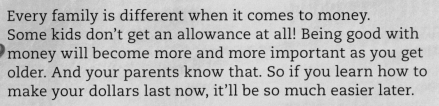

A Every family is different when it comes to money. Some kids don't get an allowance at all! Being good with money will become more and more important as you get older. And your parents know that. So if you learn how to make your dollars last now, it'll be so much easier later.

Set aside a couple dollars every week to build up your savings. Before you buy something, ask yourself if you really want it. Could you be just as happy without it? Keep track of your spending, so you always know how much money you have. And remember, little things add up a lot faster than you think!

Q I want to be on a soccer team. My moms say the uniform is too expensive and the team travels too much. How can I get them to change their minds?

A Being on a traveling sports team is a big deal. It affects the whole family, not just you. But there might be ways to make it easier. Could you carpool? Are there any businesses that donate uniforms to kids who can't afford them? Ask your parents to talk to the director of the soccer program to find out more.

If your parents still say no, you'll be disappointed, but don't let that change how you feel about soccer. Play as much as you can, wherever you can. Maybe when you're older, you can play soccer on a school team.

Q My dad has been out of work for a long time. Money's tight. It makes me worried, sad, and even a little mad too. What can I do to help out my family until he finds a job?

A The most important thing you can do is keep believing in your dad. Be positive. Tell him how much you love him, and encourage him when you can.

It might not seem like much, but simply doing what you're supposed to do can make things easier for your family. Keep up with your homework, and help out at home. Don't fight with your brothers or sisters. If you need something, it's OK to ask for it. Just try not to pester your parents about things you don't really need. They may not be able to afford extra stuff at this time.

Someday your dad will get another job, and then you can all feel good about how you pulled through this tough time together.

Tip Clip

You don't have to spend a lot of money to have a great family outing. See if your library offers discounted or free tickets to museums. Some libraries even show free movies. Parks, churches, and schools are other places to check for fun activities.

What to Say?

Q Our babysitter doesn't do any of the things she's supposed to do. She just sits around and talks to her friends. Should I tell my parents?

A Yes. Your parents are paying her to do a job, and she's not doing it. If they know what's going on, they can talk to her. Maybe she'll change her ways. If not, it might be time for a new babysitter.

 A few months ago I moved in with my grandma. I don't know where my mom is, and I haven't seen my dad in two years. Everyone I know has a perfect family. How can I keep my new friends from finding out about my messed-up family?

 Your family might not be perfect—but you know what? No one else's is either. There's no such thing. Every family has problems that others don't see. And just because your friends seem to have it easy doesn't mean it's always that way.

You can't build friendships on lies. If you know your friends well and can trust them, you should tell them the truth about your family. You don't have to tell them everything—just what you're comfortable with.

I don't like the clothes my mom buys me, but I don't want to hurt her feelings. What should I do?

 It's tough, but just be honest and tell her they're not right for you. Be nice about it. See if you can return or exchange the clothes. Your mom will probably be disappointed at first, but she'll eventually understand.

The next time you need something, ask your mom to take you on a mother-daughter shopping trip. Or shop together online. Sometimes you'll get what you want. Other times you won't. But you're growing and will need a lot of clothes in the next few years. You'll have plenty of chances to figure this one out!

Tip Clip

When you feel a problem is too big to handle by yourself, talk to a trusted adult. We all need help at times. Sometimes the only way to get help is to ask for it.

Glossary

ADHD—attention-deficit/hyperactivity disorder; a condition that causes people to have problems concentrating and sitting still

apologize—to say you're sorry for doing something

convince—to cause a person to believe or do something

divorce—the ending of a marriage by a court of law

embarrassed—feeling shame

instinct—a way of acting that a person or animal is born with and doesn't have to learn

relationship—the connection between people; the way they get along

responsible—doing what you say you will do

routine—a regular way or pattern of doing tasks

sulk—to be mad but quiet about something

support group—people with similar problems who share their stories and learn from each other

Read More

Crist, James J., and Elizabeth Verdick. *Siblings: You're Stuck with Each Other, so Stick Together.* Laugh & Learn. Minneapolis: Free Spirit Pub., 2010.

Criswell, Patti Kelley. *A Smart Girl's Guide to Knowing What to Say: Finding the Words to Fit Any Situation.* Middleton, Wisc.: American Girl, 2011.

Fox, Annie. *What's Up with My Family?* Middle School Confidential. Minneapolis: Free Spirit Pub., 2010.

Internet Sites

FactHound offers a safe, fun way to find Internet sites related to this book. All of the sites on FactHound have been researched by our staff.

Here's all you do:

Visit *www.facthound.com*

Type in this code: 9781491418581

Super-cool stuff! Check out projects, games and lots more at **www.capstonekids.com**

Index

For Louis and Helena—NL

For Lydia and Luke—PS

Snap Books are published by Capstone Press,
1710 Roe Crest Drive, North Mankato, Minnesota 56003
www.capstonepub.com

Library of Congress Cataloging-in-Publication Data
Loewen, Nancy, 1964–
  Siblings, curfews, and how to deal : questions and
answers about family life / by Nancy Loewen and Paula
Skelley ; illustrated by Julissa Mora.
      pages cm.—(Snap books. Girl talk)
  Includes index.
  Summary: "Provides tween-girl-specific information
about family life in a question-answer format"—Provided
by publisher.
  ISBN 978-1-4914-1858-1 (library binding)
  ISBN 978-1-4914-1863-5 (eBook PDF)
  1. Brothers and sisters—Juvenile literature. 2. Families—
Juvenile literature. I. Skelley, Paula. II. Mora, Julissa,
illustrator. III. Title.
  BF723.S43L66 2015
  155.43'3—dc23   2014025527

Editorial Credits
Jill Kalz, editor; Juliette Peters, designer;
Svetlana Zhurkin, media researcher;
Charmaine Whitman, production specialist

Photo Credits
Alamy: Radius Images, 10; Getty Images: Jose Luis Pelaez,
29; iStockphoto: azndc, 20, digitalskillet, 4, ferlistockphoto,
cover, Juanmonino, 8, 19; Newscom: Blend Images/
Caroline Schiff, 11; Shutterstock: Blend Images, 6, Kamira,
12, kouptsova, 27, Monkey Business Images, 24, Patrick
Foto, 22, tmcphotos, 15, wavebreakmedia, 16

Look for all the books in the series:

About the Consultant

John E. Desrochers, PhD, is a licensed
psychologist and certified school psychologist
who has worked for more than 30 years with
children and families in schools, clinics, and
private practice. He earned his doctorate in
educational psychology at Columbia University
and also holds graduate degrees in remedial
reading, behavior analysis, and marriage and
family therapy. John has numerous professional
publications and was recognized with a School
Psychologist of the Year Award by the National
Association of School Psychologists.

About the Authors

Nancy Loewen has published many books for kids.
She's a two-time Minnesota Book Award finalist
(*Four to the Pole* and *The LAST Day of Kindergarten*)
and the recipient of a Distinguished Achievement
Award from the Association of Educational
Publishers (Writer's Toolbox series). She holds an
MFA from Hamline University in St. Paul. Nancy
has two children and lives near Minneapolis.
To learn more, visit *www.nancyloewen.com*.

Paula Skelley is a blogger who writes about life,
loss, and pediatric cancer awareness. She holds a
BS in English and sociology and an MA in English
(creative writing concentration) from Minnesota
State University, Mankato. She is a mother of two
and lives in the New Hampshire Seacoast Region.

Nancy and Paula met years ago as English majors
at MSU, Mankato, and they have been friends ever
since. This is their first project together.

Printed in Canada.
092014   008478FRS15